FURTHER
OF THE
CRAMOND MICE

By Greta Walker

With illustrations by Abigail Vernon

Cramond Heritage Museum

Cramond Heritage Museum is situated at the Maltings in Cramond Village, on the edge of Edinburgh where the River Almond flows into the Firth of Forth. Visitors to the museum can discover there the fascinating history of Cramond through the ages.

Living in the museum, are eight knitted mice – The Cramond Mice – representing some of the significant eras in Cramond's long and varied history. Cramond mouse Alex welcomes children to the museum and explains that they can hunt for the rest of the mice hiding there.

Cramond Heritage Trust
The Maltings, Riverside, Cramond Village,
Edinburgh, EH4 6NY
Scottish Charity SC000754

Andrew C Walker: ISBN 978-1-5272-7451-8

Dedication

The family dedicate the publishing of this book
to the memory of Greta Walker.

Acknowledgements

Many thanks to Hazel Fey and Isla Edgar for their
knitting, crocheting and sewing skills in creating the
original Cramond Mice.

This sequel to the first book – The Adventures of the
Cramond Mice – was completed by Greta shortly before
her death in October 2019.

Husband, Andrew, took on the editing and
the illustrations were created by daughter, Abigail Vernon.

Particular thanks are due to Hannah Coulson for
her expert assistance in laying out the book and
preparing it for printing.

Chapter 1
Playing Cat and Mouse

A Siamese cat called Cockle lived in Cramond village. She was soft and silky, loving and lovely. Human creatures admired her caramel coloured fur coat and her clear blue eyes shining out of her chocolate coloured elegant face. She would purr and wind herself round the legs of those she knew and liked.

However, this gentle-seeming feline had, like most other cats, another life. Away from her cushions and kitty catty food, she was a mighty huntress, a great warrior whose array of weapons included strong sharp teeth and long needle claws.

When Cockle spied the Cramond Mice running across the road and darting into the museum through the secret door she could not believe her luck. Her eyes grew wider, a little grin crossed her face, revealing the points of her sharp teeth and she began to purr. However, she was aware that it must be teatime and decided to return to her owner's little white cottage, to plan and plot her next move whilst tucking in.

The mice were just pleased to be back in the museum after their Cramond Island adventures. Going through the secret door had changed them back from being flesh and blood furry mice into knitted mice once more.

Archibald the Victorian mouse took a key out of his pocket and locked the door. He then turned to the others and said, "Are we all in one piece after getting soaked in the Forth? Everyone check."

"My bagpipes are waterlogged," complained Scottish mouse Alex.

"Try turning them upside down and blowing hard," suggested Elsie the World War I nurse mouse.

Alex followed this advice and a stream of water ran onto the floor. She then attempted to play her pipes and after a few strange splutters and squeaks they came back to life. She gave a little jig of joy and everyone clapped.

Drest the Pict and Marcus the Roman checked their weapons and apart from being a bit rusty they were fine. Colban the medieval mouse was okay too.

Little Victorian schoolgirl Maisie had been as quiet as a mouse whilst all this checking had been going on.

"Are you okay, Maisie?" asked her

mother, Mary.

"I think I've lost Amelia," she replied, trying to hold back the tears. "She is my best friend and I need her."

She let out a little sob, then a big sob, then a great howl of despair. Amelia, her peg doll that she had clutched in her tiny paw during their adventures on Cramond Island, was now no longer in that tiny paw.

The others looked around hoping to see Amelia lying somewhere on the stone floor of the Museum. Nothing.

"When did you last have her, wee one?" asked Colban.

Maisie shook her head and managed a 'don't know' between sobs.

"There's nothing for it but to go out and look for Amelia," her mother decided. "I remember Maisie having her doll when we were on board Salty Sally. She either dropped it in the boat or after that when we crossed the road in front of the Museum."

"Well, I shall go out right now to have a look on the road, but if the doll is not there we'll have to contact my cousin Dougal," said her father, Archibald.

Dougal McDougall lived on Cramond Island with his sheep, Stanley. He was the one who had rescued them all from the flooded causeway, not much more than an hour before, and brought them home in his boat, Salty Sally.

"I won't be long," said Archibald, unlocking the secret door.

"Wait, Archibald, I'll come too," said Colban.

"Thank you, Colban, much appreciated. Lock the door behind us, someone."

Back out on the road Archibald and Colban began their search for Amelia. There were no human creatures, seagulls or dogs around. The human creatures and their canine companions had gone home for tea and the seagulls knew there would be no food for them now.

The two mice started searching near the door moving towards the steps which went down to the water. In human creature terms Amelia was about the size of a pumpkin seed. But even if she had been the size of an express train they would not have found her. Amelia had not been dropped on the road and rolled under some weed growing out of a crack in the tarmac. No, Amelia was floating in the little pool of bilge water at the bottom of Dougal McDougall's boat.

"Amelia is just not here," said Colban, as they reached the last step before the water. "Let's go back. Do you agree, Archibald?"

Reluctantly, Archibald agreed. He knew that Maisie would be upset when they came back, empty pawed, without her much loved doll.

They turned around, climbed back up the steps and looked across the road to the museum. The secret door was there but to their horror so was Cockle the cat. She was staring at it with unblinking eyes. After her tea Cockle had decided to return to the place where she had seen the mice disappear. She knew it might take some time for the mice to come out again but she was in no hurry. She was out for the night. Cockle's siege of the Museum had begun.

Now, a siege has been used for centuries as a way of defeating an enemy. Colban knew all about sieges. Everyone rushes into the castle and draws up the drawbridge when they see an enemy army approaching. The enemy army then sits outside the castle until the people in the castle run out of food and surrender. Well, that's the idea.

Colban pointed towards a bush and Archibald understood what he meant. They both ran towards the bush which now gave them more cover.

"What are we going to do, Colban?" whispered Archibald.

"I'm not very sure. We'll have to think about it. One thing is sure though, that cat is not there to pay us a friendly visit."

Chapter 2
A Siege Mentality

Inside the Museum the others were beginning to get uneasy. It had been an hour since Victorian ironworker Archibald and medieval mouse Colban had gone outside.

"I'm going to see what's keeping them," said Drest.

"No don't," urged Elsie. "I have a feeling that something is not quite right. Let's look out of the window first to see if we can see them."

"Good idea," said Alex. "We must be sensible."

Marcus was the first to scramble up onto the window ledge - followed by the others, eager to see what was happening, if anything, outside. The roadway was completely deserted. The yachts bobbed up and down in the water of the river Almond and a few seagulls flew high up in the darkening sky as an orange sun was disappearing behind the Dalmeny estate. The ducks were nowhere in sight and swan Cobb and Penn, his wife, were making their way up the river to find a suitable sleeping place for the night. A few herons on the opposite bank were doing some last-minute fishing before they too would be heading off.

Suddenly Alex saw a twitching of a branch of a bush on the opposite side of the road. The branch moved again.

"Look over there," she said, indicating the bush with her paw. "I saw some kind of movement in that bush."

They all looked. The bush twitched again and this time they saw a nose and eyes, unmistakably a mouse's nose and eyes, peeking out from between the leaves.

"Papa!" Maisie cried out. "Why is my Papa hiding in the bushes?"

"Good question, Maisie," said Elsie. "Something is definitely wrong. But what?"

"Well there is no danger as far as I can see unless there is something by the door which we can't see from here," Drest replied.

"Only one way to find out," said Marcus. "This is my plan........"

Marcus went to the Victorian schoolroom section of the museum and climbed up onto the mantlepiece of the fireplace. Here he found a ball of wool which he pushed over the edge and it fell to the floor. Alex and Mary rolled it over to the door where they were quickly joined by all the mice who gathered round awaiting their instructions. Marcus explained what he wanted them to do.

"Now, Drest, you stand behind the door ready for my signal. Once you hear me shout 'now!' open the door. Mary and Alex, as soon as the door is open I'll say 'now' for the second time and this is your signal to give the ball of wool a big push so it rolls through the door. Maisie, you stand behind Elsie. When I shout 'close,' then you know what to do, Drest."

Drest stood behind the door. Mary and Alex were ready behind the ball of wool and Maisie stood behind Elsie.

"Now!" shouted Marcus. The door swung open. "Now!" he said for the second time. The ball of wool rolled through the doorway. However, it was stopped in its tracks by what they could just see were the claws and teeth of a cat. "Close!" The door closed with a heavy thud.

It all happened in a flash but they were now only too aware of the menace that was stopping Archibald and Colban returning to the museum. They decided reluctantly that nothing was to be done that night and went to sleep.

Outside, Archibald and Colban had seen Cockle pounce, not on one of their friends, thank goodness, but on a ball of orange wool. They too decided that nothing was to be done that night. They were relieved that the others now knew why they had not returned.

Cockle of course thought that the ball of wool was a mouse but soon realised her mistake. She was disappointed at first but decided not to waste this unexpected gift and had a fine old time practising her biting and scratching techniques. After a few minutes she abandoned the now matted and tattered ball, gave herself a good wash with her delicate tongue then took up her position again by the secret door.

As dawn approached, Colban and Archibald saw Cockle get to her feet, give an enormous stretch and then stroll off. Now was their chance. Never had they run faster. Within seconds they were safely back. However, they knew that after breakfast and a sleep on her cushions, Cockle would be back too.

Chapter 3
Raw in Tooth and Claw

The Mice had gathered altogether in the school room to discuss the siege situation.

"We could stay in and only go out when the cat goes home for meals," said Elsie helpfully.

"Romans are not afraid of cats," said Marcus. "I shall not let a cat stop me doing anything I want to do."

"And Picts are definitely not afraid of cats either," added Drest. "Picts will not let a cat stand in their way."

"Listen you two. Don't be ridiculous. Cats are dangerous and can kill us," Colban interrupted. "Our situation is very serious indeed."

They had lost track of time as they discussed what to do and suddenly they were taken by surprise by the sound of a key turning in the lock of the big door into the Museum.

"It's the human creatures. Into position everyone!" shouted Alex. "And quickly!"

Immediately, all the Mice scattered, climbing up to their usual spots. Before the door was fully open there was no sign that anything had happened though they all still felt a little damp.

"There's a cat, a particularly fine cat, lurking outside the Museum," said one of the human creatures, addressing her companion.

"Well we can't worry about that now as the first visitors are due to arrive any minute," came the reply.

However, their first visitor was that cat. Cockle has seen that the big door had been left open and had decided to investigate. She walked in with a nonchalance only cats can muster. From her position on top of the counter Alex saw Cockle stroll in. She could barely control herself from blurting out 'We're doomed!'

"Here, kitty, kitty," said one of the human creatures holding out her hand whilst walking towards Cockle. She bent down and picked Cockle up.

Cockle did not like this at all. The human creature started to stroke her and rub her cheek against the soft fur. This was too much. How dare this human creature pick her up and stroke her when they had never been introduced. She gave the hand a warning bite. The other human creature had meanwhile approached and was now also stroking her. This was definitely too much for Cockle who now began to struggle free, scratching and biting with all her might.

The human creature let go and Cockle leapt to the ground and as quickly as she could, bolted out of the door.

"What a naughty cat!" exclaimed the hurt human creature. "I've got scratches all over my hand and arm. Just look."

Her companion was shocked and impressed by the red claw and teeth marks and declared, "We can't be doing with a cat like that in the Museum or even close by. Children might get hurt."

And with that she found a large brush and marched outside with it.

The Mice could hear some meows of protest and a voice shouting, "Shoo! Shoo! Don't you dare come back, naughty cat!"

And Cockle never did.

Chapter 4
Plans

When human creatures were around, the Mice had to keep very still but usually they didn't mind this too much. It gave them time to think about things. That afternoon, Maisie was thinking about her lost peg doll, Amelia. All the other mice were thinking about Maisie and how to get her peg doll back.

That evening, they were once more on their own and they gathered together to discuss the problem of the lost doll.

"We now know, thanks to Archibald and Colban, that peg doll Amelia is not outside the Museum," began Alex, "and Mary remembers seeing Amelia in the boat. Amelia must be still in the boat."

"We have to contact Dougal McDougall on Cramond Island," said Colban.

"Easier said than done," replied Mary, shaking her head. "Now that the Museum is open, we don't have enough time to go over to Cramond Island."

"How about sending a message by carrier pigeon?" suggested Elsie. "That's what happened during World War 1."

"We don't know any carrier pigeons unfortunately," said Marcus, shaking his head.

"How about climbing to the top of the Cramond Tower when it gets dark and lighting a fire? Dougal would see it and know that something was wrong," said Colban.

Colban, the medieval mouse, knew all about towers, as in medieval times towers and castles were very popular. The walls were thick and strong and built to keep any enemies out. Come too close, and approaching enemies could be shot with arrows or have hot liquid poured down upon them.

"That sounds a very good idea, Colban," said Drest enthusiastically.

"No it doesn't!" replied Elsie and Mary in unison, aghast at the idea. "You could singe your whiskers, burn yourselves or even set the whole tower alight."

"How about waving a flag from the top of the tower? Sailors use flags to send messages to each other that way," came another suggestion, this time from Alex.

"What sort of flag would we need?" asked Archibald. "I don't think there will be one which means 'peg doll lost'."

"True," said Alex, "but there is one which means 'we need to talk to you'. It is a flag with one half yellow and the other half blue."

This idea seemed to suit them all, except Drest who was really keen on the fire idea.

However, he was outvoted.

They now had to find a flag. Their thoughts turned to the Cramond Boat Club, CBC for short. The CBC club house is located just a bit further up the River Almond from the Museum. It, of course, has lots of flags that the sailors use for every eventuality - 'man overboard', 'I am on fire', 'I need medical assistance', and so on.

"I think they will keep their flags in one of their sheds," said Alex. "It will be a tight squeeze to get in under the door but I think we can manage it. Who wants to come with me?"

Archibald, Marcus and Colban volunteered to go with Alex. The flag might be heavy and bulky so they needed mice with muscles.

Out they went through the secret door, quite confidently, knowing that Cockle had been sent packing.

Chapter 5
Borrowing from the Boat Club

Within no time at all they were all outside the CBC club house. They could hear talking and laughing coming from the upstairs rooms. Obviously sailing was over for the day and the sailors were now discussing how the racing had gone.

"A pity the wind died just before Inchmickery..............I put up my spinnaker which really made the difference............I took the wrong tack........." came drifting through the air.

Tagged onto the side of the boat club were the sheds. The mice came to the first shed. Marcus and Colban volunteered to squeeze under the door whilst the other two kept watch.

It was dark in there and at first they could see nothing. Gradually their eyes did get accustomed to the darkness and they could just make out strange shaped objects in the gloom. Unfortunately, mice do not have good eyesight and in poor light they rely on their whiskers to get around. The only thing to do was to scramble up and down to find out what was there. They could detect machinery and ropes but nothing resembling flags. After much rushing around they abandoned their search and met the others waiting for them outside.

"Gosh that was a tight squeeze," said Marcus just managing to get himself back through the gap under the door.

"You're right, Marcus," agreed Colban as he joined him. "Sorry, but we have to report there are no flags in that shed. We had trouble seeing in the dark but there were definitely no flags, unfortunately."

They moved on to the next shed, hoping their luck would change. The gap under this door was even less than under the last one.

"Come on, Archibald," said Alex. "It's our turn."

"Before you go, can I just say that it might be a good idea to try and switch the light on in there. Otherwise, even if you find any flags, you'll never make out what each one is," suggested Colban.

This seemed an excellent idea.

Alex managed to go under the door and waited for Archibald. She saw his head and paws appear but that was all.

"I think I'm stuck," whispered Archibald, hardly able to talk at all.

"Give me your paws and I'll pull you," said Alex.

"And we'll give you a shove from behind," they could hear Colban say from outside.

"One, two, three, heave, Alex!"

There was a little bit of movement.

"And again," shouted Marcus. "One, two, three, heave!"

Hurrah! Archibald was through this time.

"Thank you, everyone," said the grateful Archibald, getting his breath back.

"Though how am I going to get back out?"

Now Archibald was wearing a cotton singlet, a cotton shirt, a woollen waistcoat and a thick pair of woollen trousers with long-johns underneath. It was decided that taking off some of these would make him quite a lot thinner and would allow him to make his escape. But first they had to find the flag.

It was terribly gloomy in the shed. They could just make out a cord with a plastic end hanging down from the ceiling. This was the light switch. The plan was for them both to climb up the wall and jump one at a time from the wall onto the cord. Mice are very clever climbers and Archibald and Alex were soon up the wall and found a ledge level with the dangling cord.

"I'll go first," said Archibald.

And that having been said, he made a leap into the air and grabbed the cord with all four paws. He then tried to bounce up and down to turn the light on but with no success.

"You'll need more weight," advised Alex. "I'm coming over."

She whizzed through the air like a trapeze artist and easily reached her destination, which happened to be the top of Archibald's head.

More bouncing up and down and suddenly the shed was flooded with a bright light. Now they could see ropes, ladders, a small rescue boat, sails, empty fuel cans, and yippee, hanging from the side wall was a series of pockets containing different flags.

"We've found them," shouted Alex to the others on the other side of the door.

"Well done!" came the reply.

Now they had to find the particular flag they were looking for - the yellow and blue one which meant 'we need to talk to you'.

Alex soon found it. It took both of them all their strength to pull it out of its pocket and then they let it fall to the floor.

"Hurry up, you two. Two human creatures are approaching," shouted Colban who could see a couple of sailors walking towards the sheds.

Colban and Marcus made a hasty retreat behind a weed growing conveniently out of a crack by the wall.

Inside, Archibald and Alex with great speed gathered up the flag and hurriedly scrabbled to a shadowy place just behind the door.

"Someone's left the light on in the shed. That is totally irresponsible," grumbled one of the sailors. "Don't they know about the need to conserve energy?"

"People are so careless these days," responded his companion. "We'd better switch it off."

The door opened and two large figures stood in the doorway. Whilst they were distracted locating the switch and turning off the light, our two heroes Alex and Archibald made their escape.

"Well at least I didn't have to undress," smiled Archibald as all four of the mice ran with the flag to the safety of some undergrowth.

Chapter 6
Accidental Encounter

The four of them were beginning to get their breaths back when suddenly Marcus heard a noise. It was a most disturbing noise. The faint meow of a cat.

"Listen, I can distinctly hear a cat. Can you hear it too?"

"You're right, Marcus," whispered Colban.

"That's not a normal meow," added Alex. "That is the sound of an animal in pain. Let's investigate."

"You must be mad, Alex. Cats are no friends of ours. They think of us as a tasty meal. They'd eat us for breakfast, lunch and tea if they could," warned Colban.

"I agree. Under normal circumstances cats are our sworn enemy along with foxes, stoats and weasels, birds of prey, and farmers' wives with carving knives," replied Alex. "But that meow is pitiful."

Suddenly, they heard a very quiet voice coming from deep in the dark undergrowth. They all listened intently.

"Please help me, whoever you are. I'm badly hurt. I think my leg is broken."

They looked at each other. Was this a trap? If they went into that thick dark undergrowth would they find their enemy ready to pounce? The mice thought not and definitely could not abandon an injured animal but decided to be cautious.

"Let's go back to the museum, pick up our weapons, just in case, and get the others to help," said Marcus. "We need Elsie's expertise in medical matters anyway."

"We are going to do what we can," said Alex, projecting her voice in the direction of the meows. "But first we must get help. We'll be back as soon as we can."

"Thank you, but don't be long," came the reply.

The flag was left behind, forgotten in the rush to return to the museum which they reached in a matter of a few minutes.

Chapter 7
Emergency Services

Back at the Museum, Drest, Elsie, Mary and Maisie were getting impatient for the other four to return and tried to occupy themselves by playing hide and seek. Drest had just hidden himself behind an evil looking skull, Maisie had chosen a large spade as her hiding place, Elsie was in an inkwell hole in a desk in the schoolroom and Mary was it.

She had just said, "Coming, ready or not!" when the secret door burst open and Archibald, Alex, Colban and Marcus rushed in. Immediately the others, emerging from their hidey holes, could see that something was wrong.

"We've got an emergency on our hands," panted Marcus. "There is a seriously injured cat in the bushes, who needs our help."

"I'll get my bag," said Elsie.

"Hang on a minute," intervened Drest. "Cats are dangerous as everyone keeps telling me. How do we know that this cat is any different?"

"We don't, but we believed that cat. It sounded to be genuinely in great pain. We can't ignore that," said Colban. "But as a precaution we should take our weapons."

All the mice agreed to help and quickly gathered by the secret door. Drest had his spear and shield, Colban his stick, Marcus his sword, Mary the cricket bat, and Archibald his spade. Alex didn't have a weapon but put a few little pebbles in her sporran at the last minute. Maisie with no weapon would not be allowed to get near to the cat as she was too wee. Elsie had her medical bag of course which was enough for her to carry.

Once through the secret door, they were soon by the bushes. They knew the exact spot where they had heard the cat as the flag was still there.

Their strategy was to observe the cat without it knowing they were there. Silently they went into the undergrowth, weapons at the ready. Little by little they grew closer, using leaves and branches as cover. Suddenly they saw there was a clear patch of ground ahead and lying in the middle of it was Cockle, the cat that had tried its best to catch them.

They all kept their distance but Alex was brave enough to shout, "We're back to help but first of all you have to promise not to attack us."

"I give you my solemn word that I shall not harm you. My leg is so sore and I can't stop shivering," Cockle replied in a weak voice.

Emboldened by Cockle's promise and her weakened state, the Mice began to emerge from the undergrowth. Elsie, medical bag in hand, bravely walked up to the cat.

"How did you get into this state, my dear?" she asked.

Cockle explained in a weak, meowing voice that she had been furious after being shooed away from the museum. In her anger she'd taken it out on the next thing she saw. Unfortunately, the next thing she saw was Cob, the male swan, taking a stroll in front of the Cramond Bistro. She pounced on him and he defended himself with his enormous wings and pecked Cockle with his enormous beak.

"I felt a sudden pain in my leg and crawled here," she continued.

"We must keep the patient warm," said Elsie.

"Let's get the flag," said Marcus. "We could cover her up with that."

"Good idea, Marcus. Colban and I will help you get it," said Archibald.

"Now I shall take a look at that leg," said Elsie. "Just watch those claws."

Elsie took a good look at the wound on Cockle's leg. It was deep and bleeding. She opened her bag and took out a little brown bottle, some cotton wool and some bandages. She took a little stopper out of the bottle and poured some liquid from the bottle onto a little pad of cotton wool.

"This is going to hurt, Cockle, but it will prevent infection," said Elsie as she dabbed the wound.

"Meow! Ow! Ow!" came Cockle's response to the liquid.

Next, Elsie bandaged the wound. The others had by this time returned with the flag and this was draped over the shivering Cockle.

"We need to contact your owner, Cockle. This is the best that we can do and you need urgent medical attention to see if your leg is broken," said Elsie. "Where do you live?"

"I live in the white cottage called Shell Bank, the one with the yellow door," offered Cockle. "I do so wish I was there now on my soft cushions."

Chapter 8
Where's Cockle?

Back in Shell Bank Cottage, Cockle's owner was getting worried. Totally out of character, Cockle was late for her tea which was waiting for her in her special dish. It was tasty fish morsels tonight - one of Cockle's favourites.

"It's no good, I'll just have to go out and look for her," decided her owner. And with that she put on her coat and boots and set off to do a tour of Cramond Village.

There are many hidden little gardens, alleyways and steps in the village as well as the riverside with the Museum, the Bistro and the Boat Club. She passed the now closed Blue Easel Gallery, with paintings, cards and mugs in the window. She crossed the road to see if Cockle was hanging around the Cramond Inn,

though that was highly unlikely. The Cramond Inn is major dog territory.

Cockle was not in the Cramond Inn. Her owner questioned a few of the locals standing in the doorway as to whether they had seen Cockle but unfortunately they had not.

She crossed the road again and went down the steps leading to the shore. All was quiet down there. The Bistro had sold its last delicious ice-cream of the day and was all locked up. The Museum was in darkness.

"Cockle, Cockle, where are you, Darling?" shouted her owner. "Puss, puss, puss."

Cockle's owner was now starting to panic. She quickened her pace in the direction of the Boat Club.

The mice had of course heard the approaching shouts. They have wonderful hearing.

"That's my owner," said Cockle and she began to meow weakly.

They thought it best to make a hasty retreat to the safety of the undergrowth, but could still see that Cockle was under her flag blanket meowing again and again.

Cockle's owner suddenly spied a bright patch of yellow and blue and walked up the bank towards it. As she approached she heard the faint meows of her darling Cockle.

"I'm coming, sweetheart."

A few seconds later, and Cockle was reunited with her owner. Cockle meowed now more strongly, so pleased to see her owner.

The Mice could see how tenderly the owner was taking care of her beloved cat. She gently drew back the flag blanket and immediately noticed a very neat but tiny bandage around Cockle's leg.

"This is extraordinary, Cockle. Who's been looking after you? But more to the point how did you get yourself into this state in the first place?"

Unfortunately, human creatures do not have the ability to hear animals talk and so, however much Cockle tried to explain, all her owner could hear were lots of meows. Soon Cockle's meows ceased as she became exhausted with her efforts. Her owner replaced the blanket.

"Now, Cockle, I am away to get the cat basket. I shall only be two minutes." And with that, the owner left, running as fast as she could to get the basket from Shell Bank Cottage.

The mice gathered round Cockle.

"Good luck, Cockle," said Mary and Maisie.

"All the best, you old catkin," said, Alex tenderly.

"You'll be fit and well again in no time," said Archibald, reassuringly.

"Keep well away from swans in the future, Cockle," advised Colban.

"You've been a brave cat, Cockle. As brave as any Roman Soldier I know," said Marcus.

"And, Cockle you've been as brave as any Pict I know," Drest couldn't help adding.

"Stop, all this rivalry, you two," scolded Elsie. "Now, Cockle, you look after yourself. I can hear your owner coming back so we shall make a hasty retreat."

And with that, the mice, keeping in the shadows, rushed back along the road to the Museum. Archibald opened the secret door and they were all safely back inside.

Chapter 9
All's Well That Ends Well.

"I do hope Cockle will be all right," said Elsie.

"Of course she will be," said Alex. "She got the best treatment you could give her."

"You are a wonderful nurse," said Mary. "Thank goodness you were there to help."

"We still have a big problem," said Marcus. "We haven't got Maisie's peg doll back and what's more we don't have the flag."

"We could always light a fire on top of the tower," said Drest. "That's true," said Colban.

Just then they heard a loud knock on the secret door. Immediately the conversation ceased. Everyone was silent. "Goodness me," whispered Alex. "I wonder who that is?"

The knocking came again but this time much louder and they could hear someone shouting on the other side. "Is there anyone at home?" said the unmistakable voice of Dougal McDougall.

"We're coming," responded Archibald, and all the mice gathered round him as he took the key from his pocket and opened the secret door.

"Come in dear cousin," said Archibald. "We've been trying to get in touch with you." Dougal walked in, followed closely by Stanley the sheep. "Perhaps that's the same reason why I've come," he said. "When I was cleaning out the boat I found a poor little peg doll, floating in the bilge water." "That's Amelia!" exclaimed Maisie. "My dearest doll in the world. Have you brought her?"

"Let me see," said Dougal. "She's not in this pocket, he said shaking his head, ... but she is in this one!" With a flourish he presented Amelia to Maisie. All the mice clapped.

"Thank you so much Uncle Dougal," said Maisie as she held Amelia tightly. "Yes indeed, thank you very much," said Mary.

Archibald slapped his cousin on the back and shook his hand. "You are a hero, Dougal," said Colban, and then all the mice sang:

"For he's a jolly good mousy
For he's a jolly good mousy
For he's a jolly good mousy
And so say all of us.

"And so say all of us
And so say all of us
For he's a jolly good mousy
For he's a jolly good mousy
For he's a jolly good mousy
And so say all of us."

.....

Now, you may be wondering how Cockle fared. Did her wound get infected? Is she walking with a limp? Of course not. She's totally back to her normal self, stalking and pouncing, and purring curled up on her owner's lap. However, there is one big change. The mice are now her best friends. And quite rightly so.

ALEX the SCOTTISH MOUSE

I live in the Maltings Museum. My seven friends hide in different places in the museum. Their descriptions give a clue as to where they are.

MARCUS the ROMAN MOUSE

I came to Caledonia with Emperor Septimus Severus in AD 208. Romans had been in Cramond before but we made the fort bigger and better. It is hard work unloading the supply boats that arrive up the River Almond. Please note I was not the one who dropped the Lioness in the water!

DREST the CALEDONIAN MOUSE

The Romans invaded my country, Caledonia. They called the Caledonians 'Picts' because we have pictures on our bodies. I live over the Forth in Fife. I don't want the Romans in my country and fight them when I can.

COLBAN the MEDIEVAL MOUSE

The Romans have gone. Hurrah! We are using the stones from their buildings to make our buildings. We are making a tower for the bishop. There is still a lot of fighting going on.

ARCHIBALD the VICTORIAN IRON WORKER MOUSE

There are four mills in Cramond, Dowie's Mill, Peggy's Mill, Fairafar Mill and Cockle Mill. I work at Dowie's Mill and make spades.

MARY the VICTORIAN INN MOUSE

I work at the Royal Oak Inn in Cramond Village. Travellers stable their horses and eat and sleep at the inn. Sometimes Mr Robert Louis Stevenson drops in. He drinks the beer that is brewed on this site.

MAISIE the VICTORIAN SCHOOL GIRL MOUSE

In the morning we do reading, writing and arithmetic. Sometimes we do PE when we do jumping on the spot and stretching. In the afternoon the boys learn woodwork and gardening and the girls learn sewing, housework and cooking. Now I am older I write with a pen and ink but when I was young I wrote with chalk on a slate.

ELSIE the WWI NURSE MOUSE

I work at Cramond House Red Cross Auxiliary Hospital. I care for soldiers suffering from wounds, frostbite, bad feet, fever and other diseases.